DR. BOB'S
AMAZING WORLD OF
ANIMALS
LIONS

By Ruth Owen

WINDMILL
BOOKS
New York

Published in 2012 by Windmill Books, An Imprint of Rosen Publishing
29 East 21st Street, New York, NY 10010

Editor for Ruby Tuesday Books Ltd: Mark J. Sachner
U.S. Editor: Sara Antill
Designer: Trudi Webb

Photo Credits: Cover, 1, 4–5, 6 (bottom), 8–9, 10–11, 12–13, 14–15, 16–17, 18–19, 20–21, 22–23,
24–25, 26–27, 28–29, 30 © Shutterstock; 6 (top) © FLPA.

Library of Congress Cataloging-in-Publication Data

Owen, Ruth, 1967–
  Lions / by Ruth Owen.
     p. cm. — (Dr. Bob's amazing world of animals)
  Includes index.
  ISBN 978-1-61533-547-3 (library binding) — ISBN 978-1-61533-554-1 (pbk.) —
  ISBN 978-1-61533-555-8 (6-pack)
  1. Lion—Juvenile literature. I. Title.
  QL737.C23O943 2012
  599.757—dc23

                                    2011025935

Manufactured in the United States of America

CPSIA Compliance Information: Batch #RTW2102WM: For Further Information contact Windmill Books, New York, New York at 1-866-478-0556

Contents

The Lion

Welcome to my amazing world of animals. Today, we are visiting hot **grasslands** and forests to meet some lions!

Let's investigate...

Hank's
WOOF OF WISDOM!

Lions are members of the cat family. There are 38 different types of cats.

Lions are known as big cats. Cheetahs, leopards, jaguars, and tigers are all big cats, too.

One of the ways in which lions talk to other lions is by roaring. A lion's roar can be heard 5 miles (8 km) away!

The Land of the Lion

There are two types of lions – African lions and Asiatic lions.

Asiatic lions live wild in only one place on Earth. They live in a protected park in the Gir Forest in India.

Europe

Asiatic lions live here.

Asia

Africa

India

Indian Ocean

Australia

Atlantic Ocean

African lions live in the places that are marked in orange on the map.

In the Gir Forest park, Asiatic lions are protected from hunters.

Asiatic lion

African lions

Most African lions live on hot, dry grasslands. The grasslands are covered with yellow grasses. There are also a few small bushes and trees. Some African lions live in woodland areas.

Lion Prides

Lions are the only members of the cat family to live in groups.
A group of lions is called a **pride**.

A pride of African lions may be made up of about four to six adult female lions and their babies.
There will also be one or two adult males in the pride.

Hank's
WOOF OF WISDOM!

Female lions are called lionesses. Baby lions are called cubs.

Male pride leader

The strongest male is the leader of the pride. He is also the father of all the cubs.

Lioness

Cub

Lion Bodies

Lions have big, strong bodies. They need to be strong to catch large **prey** such as zebras.

A lion can hear prey that is over 1 mile (1.6 km) away!

Adult male lions have long hair called a mane.

The lion's yellowish-brown fur is good **camouflage** among the grasses. It helps the lion hide from its prey.

A male lion's mane makes it look big and tough when it is fighting other males to become leader of a pride!

Lion Size Chart

Adult male lion

Weight = up to 530 pounds (240 kg)

Body length up to 6.5 feet (2 m)

Tail length up to 3.3 feet (1 m)

Weight = up to 375 pounds (170 kg)

Adult female lion

Body length up to 6.5 feet (2 m)

Hank's WOOF OF WISDOM!

Lions are the only cats to have a tuft on the ends of their tails.

11

What's on the Menu?

Lions are **carnivores**. Their main food is meat.

African lions hunt for large grass-eating **herbivores** such as zebras.

An adult lion will eat up to 77 pounds (35 kg) of meat in one meal!

After eating a large animal, a lion pride may not eat again for two or three days.

Lion Menu

Lions also eat these animals.

Warthogs

Antelopes

Wildebeest

Hares

Giraffes

Lions are very important to the grasslands.
They keep the numbers of grass-eating animals just right for the amount of grass available. Their leftovers provide food for smaller carnivores such as hyenas, wild dogs, and insects.

Teamwork!

African lionesses do most of the hunting for the pride.

The prey animals that lions hunt are often fast runners. So, lions use surprise and teamwork to catch their prey.

The lions circle a group of animals. They scare one animal and get it to run away from its group.

The lions chase the animal toward another lion that is hiding and waiting in the tall grass! The waiting lion pounces and pulls the animal to the ground.

Hank's
WOOF OF WISDOM!

Lions often hunt at night. In the dark, they can see up to six times better than a human!

Open Wide!

Lions have large teeth for eating meat.

A lion has 30 teeth in its mouth.

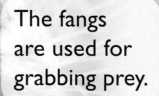

The fangs are used for grabbing prey.

These cheek teeth are used for tearing off pieces of meat. Lions don't chew their food. They swallow it in chunks!

The front teeth nibble small pieces of meat off bones.

Lions lap up water with their tongues.

A lion's tongue is rough. It uses its rough tongue to lick its fur clean.

Rough tongue

Moms and Cubs

A pregnant lioness finds a quiet place in some bushes or rocks away from the pride. In her quiet place she gives birth to between one and six cubs.

The lioness feeds the cubs milk from her body.

Cubs feeding

Spots

Their spotty coat camouflages the cubs from enemies such as leopards.

The lioness takes the cubs to join the pride when they are about 4 weeks old.
There is lots of rough play fighting in a lion pride. Now the cubs are big enough to be around the bigger, older lions.

Cute Cubs

The lionesses in a pride often give birth at the same time.
They feed milk to each other's cubs.
They also babysit for each other!

The cubs start to eat meat when they are around 6 to 12 weeks old. They still drink milk, too.

Lionesses carry their cubs in their mouths.

Cubs chase and play fight with their brothers and sisters. They also pounce on their mom's tail. It's all good practice for hunting!

Growing Up

The cubs learn how to hunt by watching and copying the adult lions.

When they are grown-up, females stay with their pride.

When a male lion is about 2 to 3 years old, he is chased from the pride by the lead male.

Young male lions live together in pairs or small groups.

When a young male is big enough and strong enough, he finds a pride. Then he fights the pride's leader and tries to take over the pride!

It's Tough at the Top!

Life as a male African lion can be tough!

A male lion may only be pride leader for two or three years. Then a younger, stronger male will take over the pride and drive him away!

The area where a pride lives is their **territory.** The pride leader tells other males to stay out of his territory. He leaves messages by scratching trees.

A male lion sends messages to other males with his urine.

KEEP OUT of my territory!

Hank's
WOOF OF WISDOM!

Asiatic lions do not live in prides. Females live in pairs with their cubs. Males only spend time with females when they **mate**.

Dangers to African Lions

Around 100 years ago, there were up to one million lions in Africa. Today, there may be only about 25,000 left!

The grasslands are being turned into farmland. If the lions lose the place where they live and hunt, they will die out.

In some parts of Africa, hunters from the United States and other countries are allowed to shoot lions for fun and sport.

Hank's
WOOF OF WISDOM!

Groups such as the World Wildlife Fund and Born Free Foundation work to help lions. Dr. Bob says if you love lions, get online and find out what you can do to help!

The Endangered Asiatic Lion

The Asiatic lion is **endangered**! There are only around 350 left in India in the Gir Forest park.

Asiatic lions once lived in many parts of India. When guns were invented, people hunted the lions until they were nearly **extinct**! Many hunters wanted a lion head as a trophy.

Asiatic lion cub

Today, it is against the law to hunt Asiatic lions.

Male Asiatic lion

Hank's
WOOF OF WISDOM!

There is a high risk of the Asiatic lion becoming extinct.

Some Asiatic lions live in zoos around the world. The zoos are breeding the lions to help increase their numbers.

Glossary

camouflage (KA-muh-flahj)
To hide an animal or allow it to blend in with its surroundings.

carnivores (KAHR-neh-vorz)
Animals that eat only meat.

endangered (in-DAYN-jerd)
In danger of no longer existing.

extinct (ik-STINGKT)
No longer existing.

grasslands (GRAS-landz)
A hot habitat with lots of grass and few trees or bushes. Sometimes it is very dry, and at other times there is lots of rain.

herbivores (ER-buh-vorz)
Animals that eat only plants.

mate (MAYT)
When a male and a female animal get together to produce young.

prey (PRAY)
An animal that is hunted by another animal as food.

pride (PRYD)
The name for a group or family of lions.

territory (TER-uh-tor-ee)
An area that an animal protects because it is where it lives and finds its food.

Dr. Bob's Fast Fact Board

One way to tell male African lions and Asiatic lions apart is by their manes. African lions normally have thicker manes that hide their ears. An Asiatic lion's ears are easier to see.

Scientists think male lions may have manes as protection for when they are fighting.

Lions have gold-colored eyes. They have a round, black pupil like a human's. Pet cats have slit-shaped pupils.

Lions in the Kalahari Desert in Africa have been seen eating melons! It's believed they were eating the fruit to get water.

Web Sites

For Web resources related to the subject of this book, go to: **www.windmillbooks.com/weblinks** and select this book's title.

Read More

Clark, Willow. *Lions: Life in the Pride*. Animal Families. New York: PowerKids Press, 2011.

Joubert, Beverly and Dereck Joubert. *Face to Face with Lions*. Face to Face with Animals. Des Moines, IA: National Geographic Children's Books, 2010.

Parker, Steve. *Big Cats*. I Love Animals. New York: Windmill Books, 2011.

Index